About this book

Many children have difficulty puzzling out letters because they are abstract symbols. Letterland's worldwide success is all about its enduring characters who give these symbols life and stop them from being abstract. In this book we meet Wicked Witch. Her story is carefully designed to emphasise the sounds that the letter 'W' makes in words. This definitive, original story book is an instant collector's classic, making learning fun for a new generation of readers.

A TEMPLAR BOOK

This edition published in the UK in 2008 by Templar Publishing
an imprint of The Templar Company plc,
The Granary, North Street, Dorking, Surrey, RH4 1DN, UK
www.templarco.co.uk

First published by Hamlyn Publishing, 1985
Devised and produced by The Templar Company plc

ISBN 978-1-84011-782-0

Printed in China

Classic LETTERLAND *Storybooks*

The Wicked Witch's Wish

Written by Jenny Samways

Illustrated by
Jane Launchbury

templar publishing

It was a wet and windy week in Letterland. The sun had not shone for days, and everyone was feeling gloomy.

"We've never had weather like this before," said the Quarrelsome Queen crossly. "It must be the work of that Wicked Water Witch. She's cast a spell on us."

Unfortunately for everyone the Wicked Water Witch was listening.

The Wicked Water Witch was FURIOUS! "Just because they are all wet, they think I cast a spell on the weather," she muttered to herself. "When I cast a spell it's *much* worse than wet and windy weather. I will show them what I can do with a spell!"

The Wicked Witch collected water beetles and weeds. She collected washing and wellington boots and wagtail's wings. Then she tossed them all into a big, black pot.

She stirred the mixture with her broomstick and whispered her spell. "Turn them all into wiggly worms!"

In a flash Letterland was covered with worms.
"Well, well, well, Quarrelsome Queen!" cackled the Wicked Witch. "You make a wonderful worm!" The Queen felt a bit queer as she wiggled about. So for once, instead of quarrelling, she just kept quiet.

Naughty Nick also felt a bit wobbly, as he wormed around. Then he had an idea.
"Let's all wiggle over and tickle the Wicked Water Witch. She hates being tickled."

So everyone wiggled up the Witch's broomstick.
They wormed their way all over her. They even wiggled their way under her hat.

"Stop, stop, stop!" cried the Wicked Witch, as she giggled helplessly. "Wait! I'll stop the spell."

She waved her broomstick and the worms disappeared.

But the Witch was still angry.
Again she stirred her pot to
cast a spell over Letterland.
"Turn them all into whales!"
she whispered.

In a flash Letterland was full of
whales.

"Water, water!" cried the whales.
"We can't live on land.
We need water!"

"This way!" called Clever Cat.
"Into the Wicked Witch's swimming
pools!"

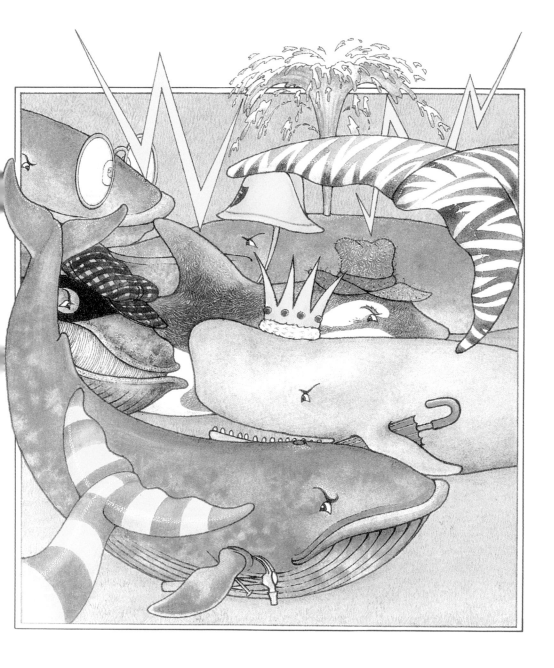

"Sssplendid idea!" hissed Sammy Snake. He slithered into one of the pools.
Was the water cold…? No!
Was it very hot…? No!
Was it wwwarm…? Yes!
It was wonderfully warm!

One by one the whales jumped in and swam to the bottom. They swam and they splashed. They had such fun…

Water went everywhere. As more of them jumped in, more water sloshed over the side. It sloshed all over the Wicked Water Witch as well.
She was getting very wet.

"Wait, wait!" wailed the Witch.
"I hate getting wet.
Just look at me. I'm soaked!"
And she was!

"Stop, stop, stop!" she cried.
"I'll stop the spell!"

She waved her broomstick again and
the whales disappeared.

By now the Witch was so cross that
she had an even worse idea.
She stirred her big, black pot and
whispered, "Turn them all into wasps!"

In a flash swarms of wasps buzzed here and there, but the wasps were angry too. They were angry with the Wicked Water Witch. They buzzed all around her.

She started to run, but the wasps chased her. She ran until she couldn't run anymore.

"Stop, stop, stop!" puffed the Witch. "I'll stop the spell!"

With a wave of her broomstick she did. The wasps disappeared.

By now the Wicked Witch had really had enough. She was wet. She was weary. But most of all she was worried because she wasn't winning.

"I will show them," she thought. "I'll turn them all to wood. Then they won't even be able to wiggle a finger." So she did.

Suddenly everyone in Letterland went stiff as wood. It was very quiet… in fact, so quiet that after a while the Wicked Witch started to wonder. "What if nobody ever talks to me again?" she thought.

The Wicked Witch started to feel
very, very lonely.
"Oh I wish I hadn't cast all
those wicked spells," she whimpered.
"I wish I could work a good spell for
a change!"

Then, for once, she had an idea that
was not wicked.

She stirred her pot, wet her broomstick,
and waved it in the air.
Then she whispered her new spell...

In a flash everything in
Lettlerland was lovely.
The weather was wonderful.
It was so warm and so beautiful that
everyone forgot to be cross with the
Witch.

"Let's all go on holiday," they cried.
So they did.

They were all so happy they even took
the Wicked Water Witch with them!

What a wonderful week that was!

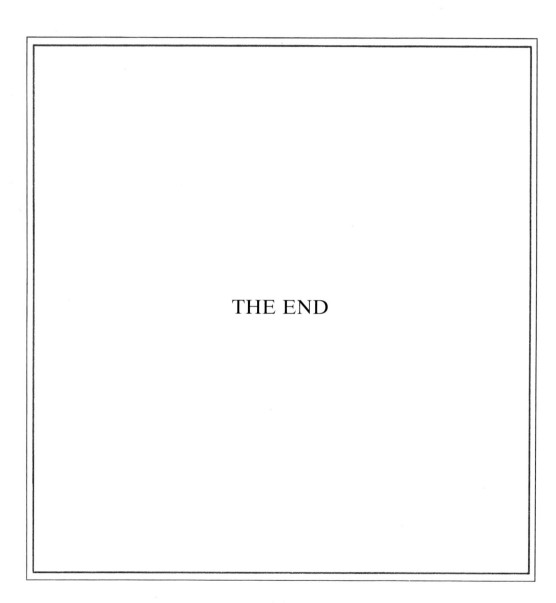

THE END